Ice Hockey Guide
Basic Rules
By Steve Robertson

Descrierea CIP a Bibliotecii Naționale a României
ROBERTSON, STEVE
    Ice hockey guide : basic rules / Steve Robertson. - București : My Ebook, 2016
        ISBN 978-606-8877-85-3

796.966

Steve Robertson

Ice Hockey Guide
Basic Rules

My Ebook Publishing House
Bucharest, 2016

TABLE OF CONTENTS

6

THE FIRST PART
THE FIELD

Article one.
THE SKATING RINK
The ice hockey is played on a field covered with ice, called "the skating rink".

Article two.
THE DIMENSIONS OF THE FIELD
a) The dimensions of the playing field must be as closely as possible to 25.925 meters in width and sixty one meters in length.

The field is surrounded with wooden boards, called ball cushions, of which height, measured from the surface of the ice, will not be bigger than 1.22 meters and not smaller than 1.017 meters.

b) The ball cushions will be built so that the surface from the interior of the field to be well smoothed and not to present any asperity that might hurt the players. The ball cushions will have a homogenous color, preferably white.

Note. *All the gates of the ball cushions will have to open toward the exterior. On the outdoor rinks, the ball cushions can be fifteen-sixty five centimeters in height.*

Article three.
THE GOALPOSTS AND NETS

a) At 3.05 meters from each extremity of the field and at the center of a red line, 5.08 centimeters wide, traced on the entire width of the skating rink and extended on the ball cushions, lie the goalposts and the regulation nets, which will be fixated in such way that they do not move during the game. If the length of the field is bigger than sixty one meters, the goalpost line cannot be placed at more than 4.575 meters from the extremity of the field.

b) The goalpost's pillars must have a diameter of 5.08 centimeters (measured in the exterior). A horizontal bar made from the same material unites at their upper extremities the two poles. The poles are 1.22 meter tall, counting from the surface of the ice at the interior part of the horizontal bar and are laid at a distance of 1.83 meters from each other, the distance counted between the interior sides of the poles.

c) Each goalpost must have a net made from a solid material, which will not allow the puck go through.

d) The goalpost's pillars, the horizontal bar and the net's frame will be entirely painted in red.

e) The red line, 5.08 centimeters wide, traced between the goalpost's pillars and extended on each side on the entire width of the field, is called "goalpost line".

f) The ice space within the goalpost, between the goalpost line and the goalpost's frame, must be painted in white.

Article four.
THE FIELD (THE SPACE) OF GOALPOST

a) In front of the goalpost is traced a rectangle called the "goalpost's space", delimited by a red line, 5.08 centimeters wide.

b) The rectangle's base is the goalpost line. The little sides are formed by two lines traced at 30.49 centimeters from the exterior side of each goalpost pillar. These little sides are 1.22 meters long. Their extremities are tied by a line parallel with the goalpost's line.

Article five.
SPLITTING THE GAME FIELD

a) The ice surface within the two goalposts is split in three parts by the two blue lines, 30.48 centimeters wide, traced parallel with the goalpost lines, at a distance of 18.3 meters from them, on the entire width of the field and continued until up the ball cushions.

On fields that are longer than sixty one meters, the blue lines must split the field between the goalposts in three equal parts.

b) The field part in which is found the goalpost is called "the defense zone" of the team that defenses this goalpost. The central part is called "the neutral zone", and the farthest part from the defended goalpost is called "the attack zone".

c) A red line called the center line, 30.48 centimeters wide, will be traced parallel with the goalpost's line, in the middle of the skating rink, on its entire width and continued until up the ball cushions.

Article six.
THE POINT AND THE CIRCLE FROM THE MIDDLE OF THE FIELD

Exactly in the center of the field, it will be made a blue point with a diameter of 30.48 centimeters. This point is the center of a circle with 3.05 meters radium, traced with a blue line of 5.08 centimeters wide.

Article seven.
LIABILITY POINTS IN THE NEUTRAL ZONE

In the neutral zone, at 1.525 meters from each blue line, are made three red dots with a diameter of 30.48 centimeters. They split the width of the field in four equal parts.

Article eight.
POINTS AND CIRCLES OF LIABILITY AT THE EXTREMITIES OF THE FIELD

a) Two red dots, with a diameter of 30.48 centimeters, are made at the half of the distance between the goalpost pillars and the nearest lateral ball cushion, and at 4.575 meters in front of the goalpost line.

b) Each of these points is the center of a circle with 3.05 meters radium, traced with a red line, 5.08 centimeters wide.

Article eight/a.
POINTS AND CIRCLES ON THE OUTDOOR FIELDS

If it is about an outdoor skating rink, the lines and points shown at the articles three, four, five, six and seven can be traced by two lines or circles, traced at the distances shown.

Article nine.
THE PLAYERS' BENCHES

a) Each field will be fitted with a place or benches for the players of the two teams. On these benches must fit minimum fourteen persons for each team. The place of the benches is nearby the center of the field and, if it is possible, near to an entrance gate that goes to the neutral zone. From the place of the benches must be a clear way to the locker rooms. The players' benches of the two teams will be placed far enough from each other.

b) On the benches can sit only the players, the leader and the coach of the team.

Article ten.
THE PENALTY BENCHES
Each field is fitted with a bench, called the penalty bench, on which can sit eight persons. It is destined for the players penalized, the penalty time clerk and the play time clerk. The penalty bench will be laid at a certain distance from the player's bench.

Article eleven.
CHRONOMETERS AND SIGNALS
a) Each skating rink must have a gong or some sound signal, for the use of the time clerk.

b) Behind each gate must be installed an electric bulb for the use of the goalpost arbiter. He lights the red bulb each time it is scored a point. In the case it is not an electric bulb, it will be used a red flag. On the skating rinks with special illumination system, a green light will indicate the end of a half time. Where it does not exist a green bulb, the whistle of the main time clerk will indicate the end of the half time.

Note. *If it is possible, each skating rink must have an electric chronometer, which will indicate to the spectators, players and referees the duration of the played game.*

A point cannot be counted as scored, if the green light does not lights or if the time clerk whistled the end of the match while the puck was in the air.

Article twelve.
THE LOCKER ROOMS AND THE ILLUMINATION OF THE FIELD
a) Each skating rink must have lockers in good state, a medical office of first aid and showers.

13

b) A special locker room will be reserved for the referees.

c) No one, except for the delegate of the Local Commission or the Organizing Commission, can enter in the referees' locker.

d) The field must have a lights installation, which will allow the players and the spectators to see easily the game during the night.

THE SECOND PART
THE TEAMS

Article thirteen.
THE COMPOSITION OF THE TEAMS

a) A team, during the game, is composed of six players registered at that association (collective).

b) Each player will wear on the back of his t-shirt an order number, in a dimension of maximum25.4 centimeters and of a distinct color from the t-shirt.

Article fourteen.
THE CAPTAIN OF THE TEAM

a) Each team has to assign a team captain. He is the only player authorized to discuss with the referees all the problems of interpretation over the rules of the game, regarding the stages that intervene during a match.

The team captain will wear the letter C, stitched on the front of his t-shirt. The size of this letter will be, approximately, of 7.62 centimeters and will have a visible color, other than the one of the t-shirt.

b) Each team must have, during the entire game, a captain on the field. If the captain player is not on the field, his replacer bears all the rights of the captain.

The surrogate captain will have to wear on his t-shirt the letter A (also 7.62 centimeters tall, visible size and color).

c) The name of the captain of the team and of his replacer will be communicated, before the game, to the game referees and to the secretary referee which has the job to make the list.

d) The goalkeeper or his replacer cannot receive the job of captain or captain replacer.

Article fifteen.
THE TEAMS' PLAYERS

a) At the beginning of each game, a team cannot have more than fifteen players equipped, of which two goalkeepers. Only these players are authorized to be part of the game.

b) A list with the names and numbers of the players must be entrusted to the secretary referee, specially appointed before the game. No change or addition is authorized after the beginning of the game, except for the goalkeepers.

c) A team cannot have on the field more than one goalkeeper. The goalkeeper can be called back or replaced by another field player, but this player does not enjoy the rights the goalkeeper has.

d) No other player is authorized to wear the goalkeeper equipment, beside the goalkeeper.

Note. *The teams are authorized to have a back-up goalkeeper and use him as they please. But this goalkeeper cannot replace the tenured goalkeeper, if he received a match penalty.*

Article sixteen.
THE FORMATION OF THE TEAMS AT THE BEGINNING OF EACH HALF TIME

a) Before starting the game and before each half time, the leader or the coach of the team must point to the referees or the secretary referee, the name of the players that start the half time. The players will be prepared by their responsible to start the game, at the request of the referee.

16

No change can produce in the composition indicated to the referees or the secretary referee, before the game starts actually. In the case of breaking this rule, a minor penalty will be applied to a player of the team that made the mistake.

Article seventeen.
BALANCING THE TEAMS
If a team cannot align six players anymore, as the result of some accidents and after all the fifteen players indicated, except for the goalkeepers, have been part of the game, the adversary will have to withdraw from the game as many players so that both teams remain with an equal number of players.

Article eighteen.
REPLACING THE PLAYERS
a) The replacement of the players is authorized in any moment under the condition that the players which leave the ice to be on the players' bench, before their replacers to go on the field.

b) A player which suffered a penalty and which is on the penalty bench, at the end of the punishment and before being replaced must pass over the ice to go on the players' bench.

c) In the case of breaking this rule, it will be applied a minor penalty to the replacement player.

Article nineteen.
THE INJURED PLAYERS
a) If a player is injured (other than the goalkeeper) and is forced to leave the ice during the game, he can draw back from the game, being replaced, but the game must go on without the teams leaving the ice.

b) If the goalkeeper is hurt, it will be conferred ten minutes time-out, for him to rally. The minutes are counted from the moment he leaves the ice.

c) If it is necessary to be replaced by another goalkeeper, it will be afforded five extra minutes. The replacement goalkeeper is bound to all the rules and benefits of all the rights that the goalkeeper has. He is authorized to wear the full gear of the goalkeeper.

d) If the goalkeeper is injured, the players are authorized to leave the field announcing the referee, but they will be ready to restart the game immediately, at the request of the referee.

e) If a penalized player is injured, he can go straight to the locker rooms, without passing through the penalty bench. He can be replaced after passing the penalty time, even though he is not on the penalty bench.

The leader or the coach who makes the replacement will be careful not to make the replacement before the penalty time is over.

f) In the case of breaking this rule, it will be applied a minor penalty to the replacement player.

g) If, because of an injury, a player cannot continue the game and neither he can return at the players' bench, the game will not be stopped until the team from which the injured player is part of has the puck.

If the team from which the injured player is a part of has the puck, the game can be stopped immediately, except for the case it is in a favorable situation to score a point. The referee will let the phase continue, without interrupting the game.

Note. *If a player is badly injured, the referee can stop the game immediately, no matter who has the puck.*

THE THIRD PART
THE EQUIPMENT

Article twenty.
THE HOCKEY STICKS
a) The hockey sticks must be made out of wood, well smoothed.

b) The length of a hockey stick cannot overcome 134.62 centimeters, calculated from the top of the handle to the stick's angle and 37.465 centimeters from the angle of the stick to the end of the blade.

c) The blade of the hockey stick cannot be longer than 7.62 centimeters. The goalkeeper's hockey stick blade cannot be wider than 8.89 centimeters, except for the angle, which can reach even a width of 11.43 centimeters.

d) It will be applied an unfair attitude penalty to the player who will use a hockey stick overcoming the dimensions provided by this statute, except for the goalkeeper.

e) It will be applied a minor penalty to the goalkeeper which uses an irregular sized hockey stick.

Article twenty one.
THE SKATES
a) The players will use special hockey skates.

b) It is forbidden using speed skates, show or any other model that can produce accidents.

Article twenty two.
THE GOALKEEPER'S EQUIPMENT

a) Except for the skates and the hockey stick, the entire equipment of the goalkeeper must serve for protecting his body and head. No object from his equipment must facilitate defending the goalpost.

Note. *The gloves cannot have any additional material intertwined between the thumb and the index, to cover the glove's opening when the hand is opened, and the fingers are scattered. This kind of "pocket", from any material, is forbidden.*

b) The width of the goalkeeper's fenders must not overcome 25.4 centimeters for each of them, when they are attached on the leg.

c) It will be applied a minor penalty to the goalkeeper who uses an irregular equipment, and the game will be interrupted, until the goalkeeper gets legit.

Article twenty three.
THE PROTECTION EQUIPMENT

The entire protection equipment, except for the goalkeeper's fenders, the players' gloves and helmets, must be worn under the t-shirt and socks. It will be applied a minor penalty to the player that continues to bend this rule, after the referee gave him a warning.

Note. *All the players that break this rule, except for the goalkeeper, must not be allowed to take part to the game, before they comply with the referee's observations regarding the equipment. The wired masks cannot be used, the exception being the goalkeeper. The small dimensions mask for the players wearing glasses is authorized, under the condition it is not harmful through its construction.*

Article twenty four.
EQUIPMENT THAT CAN CAUSE ACCIDENTS
Using metal fenders or any other material, that can cause injury to a player, is forbidden.

Article twenty five.
THE PUCK
The puck must be made of vulcanized rubber, having a cylindrical shape, with the height of 25.4 millimeters and the diameter of 7.62 centimeters.

Note regarding the third part. *Any measurement of the equipment shown in this part must be made before the game or between the two pauses, without delaying the beginning or the deployment of the game.*

THE FOURTH PART
PENALTIES

Article twenty six.
PENALTIES
All the penalties are calculated in effective game time and are the following:
1. Minor penalty.
2. Major penalty.
3. Penalty for irregular attitude.
4. Match penalty.
5. Penalty kick.
Note. *If a player makes a mistake when the game is stopped, he will be punished with the same penalty as during the game.*

Article twenty seven.
MINOR PENALTY
Minor penalty means eliminating the player that made a mistake for two actual game minutes. Exception is eliminating the goalkeeper.

Article twenty eight.
MAJOR PENALTY
a) The first major penalty applied to a player during the game, except for the goalkeeper, is five minutes elimination, without replacement allowed.

b) The second major penalty applied to a player during the game, except for the goalkeeper, is elimination from the game for fifteen minutes, a replacement being allowed after five minutes though (major penalty plus penalty for unfair attitude).

c) The third major penalty applied to a player, except for the goalkeeper, is elimination from the game for the rest of the match, a replacement being authorized though after five minutes (major penalty plus match penalty, for unfair attitude).

Article twenty nine.
PENALTY FOR UNFAIR ATTITUDE
a) Penalty for unfair attitude means elimination from the game of the player that made the mistake, except for the goalkeeper, for ten minutes. An immediate replacement of the grounded player is allowed though.

b) A match penalty for unfair attitude means the elimination from the field of the player that made a mistake, for the rest of the match. An immediate replacement of the grounded player is authorized.

Article thirty.
MATCH PENALTY
a) A match penalty means eliminating the player for the rest of the match. The punished player must go immediately to the lockers. Replacement of a punished player is authorized after ten minutes of playing in the case of the article eighty one and after five minutes in the case of the article eighty, seventy one (b), seventy seven and seventy eight.

Note. *The indications regarding the extra punishments and replacements can be found at the articles seventy seven, eighty and eighty one. All the extra punishments are applied to the player that is appointed by the leader or the coach, through the team captain that is on the field.*

24

b) A player that suffered a match penalty cannot be part of another game, before the mistake is adjudicated by the Local Hockey Commission, or in the case of a tournament, by the Organization Commission, on which attribution falls adjudicating the case.

Note. *The referees must report to these Commissions any match penalty, noting into the report the conditions in which the mistake happened. This report will be written immediately after the game.*

Article thirty one.
PENALTY KICK

a) A "penalty kick" is executed as the following: the puck is put on the blue line of the third from the defense of the team that made the mistake. A random player (not penalized in this moment) plays the puck at the referee's whistle and tries, without interrupting the action, without stopping, to score a point.

b) The goalkeeper must remain in his goalpost field, until the moment when the adversary starts to play the puck. From this moment, the goalkeeper can try stopping the puck with all his means, excepting throwing the hockey stick, because, in this case, it will be awarded a point.

Note. *See article sixty seven.*

c) Immediately the player attacking started to play the puck, it must be maintained in movement and driven without stopping toward the opposite goalpost. When the player in attack hits, his action is over. A point cannot be scored immediately, after one rejected puck.

d) A player against whom it was committed an error that brings the sanction of a penalty kick and which is assigned to execute the hit, but made himself, in the same phase, a mistake (either before, either after it was granted the penalty kick), can execute it before starting his own punishment.

e) During executing the penalty kick, the players of the two teams must draw off toward the lateral ball cushions of the field.

f) If during executing the penalty kick a player from the team in defense stops or steals in any way the attention of the one executing the kick, in this way the kick being failed, it will be granted a second ry. The referee will punish the player that intervened in the phase, with a penalty for unfair attitude.

g) When it is scored a point from a penalty kick, the puck will be put in game from the center of the field as it is done at the beginning of the game or after scoring a point. If the point is not scored the puck will be put in game at one of the points situated at the extremity of the field, in the area where it was executed the penalty kick.

h) If it is scored a point from a penalty kick, the player that made the mistake will not be penalized anymore, except for the case when his mistake will draw a major penalty or of match, which will have to be executed. If it is not scored a point, it will be applied the appropriate penalty for the mistake the player has made.

i) The necessary time for executing a penalty kick will not be taken from the game time or from any eventual extension.

Article thirty two.
PENALTIES AGAINST THE GOALKEEPER

a) The goalkeeper to whom is applied a minor penalty, does not go on the penalized players' bench, but is replaced by a field player designated by the leader or the coach of the team he is part of. The mentioned player takes the punishment for the goalkeeper.

b) If a goalkeeper makes a mistake that normally would attract against him a major penalty, he does not execute the punishment. It is replaced with a penalty kick, without any other extra sanction.

c) If a goalkeeper makes a mistake that brings a second penalty kick, it will be applied to him a match penalty for unfair attitude, and after the penalty kick has been executed, his place will be taken by a player from the team that participated at the game (but not by a goalkeeper that has been equipped and figured as such on the list made before the game).

The player that takes the goalkeeper's place can use the entire equipment of the one eliminated, being granted fifteen minutes for equipping.

d) If against a goalkeeper is announced a match penalty, his place will be taken by a field player that participated at the game, in the same conditions as at the c) paragraph.

e) If a goalkeeper makes a mistake that attracts a penalty for unfair attitude, this sanction will be taken by a field player found on ice in the moment of the violation.

f) If the goalkeeper is punished with a match penalty, his place will be taken by a field player that participated at the game in the moment of the violation and which will be allowed to wear the goalkeeper's equipment. For this purpose will be awarded a fifteen minutes break for equipping the new goalkeeper. The back-up goalkeeper found on the players' bench cannot replace the penalized goalkeeper.

g) If the goalkeeper leaves the area of the goalpost to be part of a discussion with the referees or adversaries, he will be punished with a minor penalty.

Article thirty three.
VARIOUS PENALTIES

a) If a third player of the team is penalized, while other two punished players are on the penalization bench, his punishment starts the moment when it is over the punishment of one of the players found outside. Still, a third penalized player goes on the penalization bench and he is replaced with a player before the moment it starts his punishment.

b) In the case when a team has three players punished at the same time, in the virtue of the rule that allows replacing the third punished and a replacer is found on the field for the third player penalized, no player from the ones punished can enter on the field, after the time of the punishment has passed, if the game is not stopped and if the one that replaced had not left the ice.

If the game is stopped and the surrogate player has taken his place on the bench, the one that finished the punishment can enter into the game.

c) When it must be applied the rule by replacing the third penalized, the referee will tell the punishment time clerk, that the one punished cannot enter on the field until when the game is stopped, and the surrogate has taken his seat on the players' bench.

d) When two punished players finish in the same time the penalty, the team captain will indicate to the referee whom of them enters first into the game, and the referee warns for this purpose the penalty time clerk.

e) When the punishment of two players ends in the same time, the team can have on the field more than four players and the penalty time clerk will authorize the player that was indicated by the referee to reenter the field.

Article thirty four.
SIGNALIZING THE PENALTIES
a) If the player of a team that does not own the puck in that moment makes the mistake that draws a minor penalty, major or of match, the referee will indicate with his finger the guilty player. Immediately the phase is over, the referee will penalize this player.

b) If from such a phase is scored a point, the guilty player of the defense team will not be punished anymore, if it is about a minor penalty. If it is about a major or match penalty though, it will be applied.

c) The referee will stop the game immediately if the mistake is made by a player of the team that leads the puck.

d) If a player that makes a mistake makes other deviations in the same phase, before or after the referee stopped the game, the penalties will be cumulated.

THE FIFTH PART
THE REFEREES

Article thirty five.
CHOOSING THE REFEREES

a) For each game are necessary: two referees, one time clerk, one penalty time clerk, a secretary referee and goalpost referees.

b) For all the hockey games will only be used referees that are on the list of the Central Hockey Commission.

Article thirty six.
THE GAME REFEREES

a) The referee leads the game and controls all the referees (secretary, time clerk) and all the players during the match. The referee stays on the field until the last player leaves the ice.

b) The referees will wear different equipment than the players. It is forbidden for a leader or a player, except for the captain, to talk to the referee before or during the game.

c) The referee must be neutral.

d) The referee must call the teams on the field, at the beginning of the game, as well as at the beginning of each new half time. Any delay in starting a game, must be noted by the referee on the arbitration chart, along with the reasons of the delay.

e) The referee must check at the beginning of the game, if all the players use the appropriate equipment.

f) The referee must check at the beginning of the match if the time clerk, the penalty time clerk, the goalpost referees and the secretary referee are in their places and check if the time measuring system and signals work appropriately.

g) The referee has the duty to apply the sanctions stated in this regulation and take a definitive decision when it is contested a point, after he will check with the goalpost referee.

h) The referee must announce to the secretary referee the points scored, and to the penalty time clerk all the sanctions made.

i) The referee must check if the players' benches of the two teams are at enough distance from each other.

j) The referee must stop the game at each violation regarding the offside rule at the blue line, at the center line or any violation of the rule regarding to "forbidden release".

k) If a referee leaves the ice for any reason, the game is considered interrupted.

l) If on an act of God situation the referees assigned do not present to the match, the delegates of the two teams can agree over choosing other referees. If they cannot agree over other referees, the game will be lead by a player, by each team.

m) If the secretary-referee or the goalpost referee does not come to the match, they will be replaced by surrogates.

n) If because of an accident or because of illness, a referee can no longer continue working, the second referee will lead by himself.

o) The referee must check the identity of the player, asking for their identity cards. This formality is made before being signed the arbitrage chart.

Article thirty seven.
ARBITRAGE IN TWO
The international games are led by two referees with equal rights. In case of different opinions, the definitive decision will

be given by the referee that is found closer to the phase. The championship games will be led also by two referees. Only in exceptional cases will lead only one referee.

Article thirty eight.
THE GOALPOST REFEREES

a) A goalpost referee must stand behind the each goalpost. The goalpost referees cannot be members of the teams that play and cannot be changed during the game, only when it is determined that one of them takes unjust decisions. In this case, the referee will point a replacer.

b) The goalpost referees will stand behind the goalpost, in a special cage if it is possible, so that they can accomplish their task in good conditions. They will not change the goalpost during the match.

c) Before awarding a point, the goalpost referee must establish precisely if the puck passed entirely by the goalpost's poles or if it passed entirely the goalpost line. His decision is simple: "point" or "it is not a point". In case of "point", he will light the red bulb or will flutter the red flag visibly. If it is not a point, he will not make any sign.

Article thirty nine.
THE PENALTIES TIME CLERK

a) The penalties time clerk must keep an exact inventory of all the punishments given by the referee, including the name, the error made and the length of the penalty.

b) The penalty time clerk will control the length of each penalty. He will have to indicate, at demand, to the player punished, how much more time does he has to stay on the penalty bench.

c) The penalties time clerk must sign at the end of the game the list of the penalized, which he gives to the referee, to be attached to the arbitrage chart.

Article forty.
THE SECRETARY REFEREE

a) Before starting the game, the secretary referee must build a list with the formation of the players from the two teams. He will note on the list, past the name of the team captain, the letter C, and past the replace captain, the letter A. The chart completed with the names of the players and with their identity cards is given to the referee before the match.

b) The secretary referee will keep an evidence of the scored points, writing down the name of the player that obtained the point. He will also write down the minute when the replacing goalkeeper enters.

c) The secretary referee will receive from the penalty time clerk the list of the punishments, which he will attach to the arbitrage chart. He will present to the referee, at the end of the game, the chart to be signed. The official delegate transmits the arbitrage chart to the Town Commission, Regional Commission or to the Central Hockey Commission, as it meets the case.

d) In case it is not assigned a secretary referee, these formalities will be made by one of the referees.

Article forty one.
THE GAME TIME CLERK

a) The game time clerk records the beginning, the end and all the half times of the game.

b) The game time clerk will indicate to the referee the start of the game and each half time, as well as the finish of the ten minutes breaks. After this signalization, the referee starts or ends the game. The game time clerk signalizes through whistling the end of each half time or the eventual extensions.

c) In case of contestation over the game time, the match referee is the judge of the contestation. The trial is made right away.

THE SIXTH PART
GAME RULES

Article forty two.
THE GAME'S DURATION
a) A match lasts three half times, each of twenty minutes effective playing, separated by a ten minutes break.

b) The team that scores the most points in these half times is the winner of the game.

c) During the breaks, the ice must be swabbed.

Article forty three.
"EQUAL" GAME
If after the three half times of twenty minutes each the result is equal, the match is counted as "equal".

Article forty four.
THE BEGINNING OF THE GAME
a) The game starts in each half time through an undertaking in the center of the field.

b) The team on which field is played the game, the host team, has the right to choose the goalpost they will defend at the beginning of the game. The team will change the goalpost at each half time or extension.

Article forty five.
HOW TO SCORE A POINT

a) A point is scored when the puck, sent by the hockey stick of a player attacking, passes through the goalpost's poles, under the horizontal bar. The puck must come from the front of the goalpost and to pass entirely over the red line that is marked on the ice from one pole to another and which has the width equal with the diameter of the goalpost's poles.

b) A point is scored when the puck enters the goalpost, after it has been touched by a player in defense. The attack player that touched, the last, the puck, is considered to have marked the puck.

c) If a player in attack hit the puck with his foot and then the puck is touched by a defense player, entering into the goalpost, it is awarded a point. The player that hit the puck with his foot is considered to have scored the point.

d) If the puck hit with the hockey stick by a player in attack touches any part of the body of a player from the same team, it is awarded a point. It is not awarded a point in the case the puck would have been hit with the foot or the hand and after touches a player from the same team.

e) If the puck enters into the goalpost, being hit a player and in its trajectory it hit the referee, it is not awarded a point.

f) If a player sends in a correct way the puck in the goalpost's space and from here it is sent into the goalpost, it is awarded a point.

g) Any point scored in other conditions than the ones stated before, is annulled. Each point is considered in favor of that team and is written at the column of the player that scored.

Article forty six.
PLAYING REFUSAL

a) If one of the teams found on ice refuses to play after the referee ordered the beginning or continuing the game, will receive from the referee a thirty seconds recess to start the game or abandon the match.

b) After thirty seconds, if the team refuses to play, the referee will give a minor penalty against a player from the team that made the mistake. If the team still refuses to play after this sanction, the referee will declare winner the other team.

c) If a team does not present on ice in five minutes from the referee's whistle, will be declared loser by forfeit.

Article forty seven.
ENGAGEMENTS

a) The referee puts the puck into the game throwing it between two players that are standing in front of each other, each faced toward the adversary goalpost. The players are standing at a hockey stick length from each other. The blade of the hockey stick is put on the ice.

No player can be at less than three meters than the two players found in engagement. The team colleagues will sit one-sided or in the back. No player can overcome the position on the field of the two players that are engaging.

The sticks of the ones that engage are put in the back of the engagement point. The game starts the moment when the puck touches the ice. In the case this rule is not respected, the engagement will be made again.

b) The referee will not whistle for restarting the game. The time is counted from the moment the puck touches the ice.

c) When a player breaks this rule the second time, the referee will sanction him with a minor penalty.

d) If a mistake is made in his area of attack by a player from the attack team, the engagement is made at the nearest point of engagement from the neutral zone.

e) If a mistake is made in the same time by two players of the two teams, the engagement is made where the mistake has been made or where the game has been stopped; this is in the case when it is foreseen that the game must continue until finishing the game phase, and if it is not fixated especially by the regulation another point.

f) If the game is stopped when the puck is found between the engagement points situated at the margin of the field and the ball cushions found behind the goalpost, the engagement is made at one of the points from the part where the game was stopped.

g) No engagement can be made at less than 4.175 meters from the goalposts or the lateral ball cushions.

h) If a point has been scored irregular, after the puck touched the referee found in the defensive zone (when the puck is at one of the players of the defending team) the engagement is made at one of the points from the defensive area. But if the puck was in the possession of an attack player, the engagement is made at the nearest point from the neutral zone.

i) If the game has been stopped for a reason unspecified in this regulation, the engagement is made from where the puck was in the moment the game was stopped.

Article forty eight.
THE PASS

a) The puck can be passed by any of the players, to any team colleague, inside any of the three zones. The puck cannot be passed forward, by a player found in a zone, to another colleague found in another zone. Exception is the player found in the defensive area, which can pass to his colleague found in the neutral zone, but not farther than the middle of the field. In the case when it is made such an error, it will be made an engagement from the place of the pass.

b) If the puck passed touches the body, the stick or the skates of a team colleague that is not found in offside, the pass is considered good.

c) The player that touches the puck is considered to be the player that owns the puck.

d) If a player found in the neutral zone is preceded in the attack area by the puck came from the neutral zone, he has the right to touch the puck in any part of the attack zone, outside the case it can be applied the rule of "forbidden evolution".

e) If a player that is found in the area where a pass has been made is preceded by the puck in another area, he has the right to take the puck in the area where he is now, outside the case when it is applied the rule of "forbidden evolution".

f) If a player in attack is found in the attack area and if he passes the puck back, meaning in the direction of his own goalpost, in this case an opposite player can touch the puck, but he has to be preceded by it if he passes from the neutral zone to the attack zone.

Article forty nine.
PUCK HIT WITH THE FOOT
The puck can be hit with the foot in any area, but a point scored with the foot by a player in attack, will not be awarded except for the case when the puck sent this way, enters into the goalpost touched by a player from the team found in defense.

Article fifty.
STOPPING AND THROWING THE PUCK BY HAND
a) If a player, other than the goalkeeper, catches the puck into his palm, the referee will stop the game and will make an engagement. The goalkeeper that holds the puck into his hand more than three seconds will receive a minor penalty.

b) The goalkeeper cannot hold intentionally the puck interrupting the game. He must not throw the puck forward and neither to hide it intentionally into his equipment or to gather snow in front of the goalpost, to stop scoring a point. It will be applied a minor penalty to the goalkeeper that will break this rule.

Note. *If the puck thrown by the goalkeeper forward is caught by an adversary player, the referee will admit the continuation of the phase. If from this situation is scored a point, it will be awarded without any penalty being applied to the goalkeeper. If the point is not scored, the game will continue, without penalties.*

c) The player that lifts during the game the puck with his hand will receive a minor penalty.

d) A player is allowed to stop with open hand the puck that is coming through the air, but to let it fall on ice. The player can also put by hand the puck on the ice, if in the referee's opinion, by this action he did not passed intentionally the puck to a colleague. If it made a mistake in this last case, it will be made an engagement from the place of the mistake.

Article fifty one.
FORBIDDEN EVOLUTION

a) For applying this rule, the center line divides the field in two halves. If a player of a team, equal or superior in numbers to the other team, sends the puck from the half that belongs to him, beyond the adversary goalpost line, the game must be stopped, being made an engagement at one of the points of the defense third of the team that made the mistake. In the case the puck enters the adversary goalpost, it is awarded a point.

b) If the puck was sent by a player of the team inferior in numbers, to the other team, the game must continue without stopping or awarding an engagement.

c) If a "forbidden evolution" is made after an engagement, it is not stopped the game neither engagement.

d) If, in the referee's opinion, a player of the adversary team, except for the goalkeeper, had the possibility to stop the puck before it passed the goalpost line, but did not do it, the game is not stopped and neither is given an engagement.

e) If the puck, before crossing the goalpost line touches a player from the adversary team, his skate or hockey stick, the game is not stopped and neither is given an engagement.

f) If, in the referee's opinion, a player that tried to pass to a colleague, and the puck, without touching anyone, crosses the adversary goalpost line, the game is not stopped and neither is given an engagement. In this case, only the player that passed is the only one from his team that has the right to first play the puck.

g) If the referee makes a mistake, stopping the game for "forbidden evolution" made by a team inferior in numbers to the adversary team, the engagement is made at 1.525 meters in the interior of the defensive zone of the team superior in numbers and exactly in the middle of the field, counted in width.

h) In the case the referee makes a mistake by stopping the game in the same conditions like the g point, the teams being at a tie as number of player, the engagement is made in the neutral zone, at the farthest point from the goalpost of the team that first had the puck.

Note. *For the good interpretation of this rule, the "forbidden evolution" is counted in the moment when the puck passes the goalpost line.*

Article fifty two.
OFFSIDE

a) A player is in offside when he passes completely, with both his skates, the decisive line for each case. The offside is determined after the position of the player's skates, without taking into account the position of his hockey stick.

b) If, in the referee's opinion, it was committed a voluntary offside, the engagement will happen at one of the defensive points of the team that made the mistake.

Note. *This rule does not apply to the team that is smaller in numbers than the other team. In this case, the engagement is made in the place of the mistake.*

Article fifty three.
PLAYER IN FRONT OF THE PUCK IN THE ATTACK ZONE

a) The player in attack is not allowed to enter in front of the puck in the attack zone.

b) If it is broken this rule, the game will be stopped, being made an engagement in the neutral zone, at one of the points close to the attack area of the team that made the mistake.

Note. *The player that owns the puck and passes this way the attack line in front of the puck he is leading, is not counted as offside.*

c) If an attack player passes in front of the puck he is leading into the attack area, and the puck is stopped by a defense player on the blue line or close to it, will not be counted as an offside, the game continuing without any interruption.

d) If a player passes the puck from the neutral zone in his defense zone, and in the defense area is found a player of the adversary team, it is not whistled an offside, the game continuing also without interruption.

Article fifty four.
THE PUCK IN MOVEMENT

a) The puck will be held in continuous movement.

b) A team owning the puck is obliged to play the puck in the direction of the adversary goalpost, outside the cases when it is stopped by the adversary players to do this. It is allowed though to be made a single pass in the back of their own goalpost, in the case when this rule is broken it will be made an engagement at the nearest point from the goalpost of the team that made the mistake.

The referee must tell the captain or his replacer the reasons that determined the punishment. The second breaking of this rule by the same team, during the same half time, draws a minor penalty for the mistaking player.

c) The player, except for the goalkeeper, that intentionally holds the puck into the ball cushion, no matter by which means, will receive a minor penalty. It is not taken into the consideration the case when he is pushed by an adversary.

d) A player found in front of his defense area is not allowed to pass or lead the puck back into his defensive area, intending to delay the game. In the case of not respecting this rule, it will be made an engagement in the nearest point, in the defense area of the mistaking team.

Article fifty five.
PUCK SENT INTENTIONALLY OUT OF THE FIELD

The player that delays the game by sending intentionally, no matter by what means, the puck outside the ice surface that the game is disputed on, will receive a minor penalty.

Article fifty six.
PUCK OUT OF THE FIELD'S LIMITS

a) If the puck exits the field on one of the extremities or because of an obstacle found on top the ice, except for the ball cushions, goalposts or nets, the game will be stopped and will be made an engagement in the place where the puck was in game the last time, or from the place where it deviated.

b) If the puck remains in the net that covers in the exterior the goalpost and cannot be player forward, the referee will stop the game and will make an engagement at the nearest point. In the case the puck was sent into the net (at the exterior) by an attack player, the engagement will be made in the neutral area.

c) The goalkeeper that intentionally puts the puck in the exterior net of the goalpost with the intention to delay the game will be punished with a minor penalty.

Article fifty seven.
THE PUCK CANNOT BE SEEN
If during a immixture or if a player falls involuntary over the puck and it is not seen by the referee, the game will have to be stopped immediately. It will be made an engagement in that spot.

Article fifty eight.
THE PUCK TOUCHES THE REFEREE
The game will not be stopped if the puck touches the referee (see the note of article forty five).

Article fifty nine.
UNFAIRNESS TOWARD OFFICIALS
a) To the player, that during the game has an unfair attitude toward anyone (referee, adversary, by-stander) will be applied an unfair attitude penalty.

b) In the case when a coach or leader of one of the teams has an unfair attitude toward anyone (referee, the players of the adversary team etcetera), the referee will be able to state for the guilty to leave immediately the players' bench, making a report to the Central Hockey Commission, over the case.

c) If a coach or team leader is eliminated from the players' bench after the referee's disposition, he cannot stand nearby, intending to lead his team's play under any form.

d) In the case the referee cannot identify exactly the player, coach or the leader of the team that made a mistake from the ones stated at the points a and b, he can apply a minor penalty to a player of the team that made the mistake. This player will be pointed by the team captain.

Article sixty.
THE OFFENCE OF THE REFEREE
a) If a player has an inappropriate attitude toward a referee, it will be applied an unfair attitude penalty, and in case of relapse, will be eliminated from the game.

b) If a coach or a team leader has a completely unfair attitude toward the referee, will be punished immediately with the interdiction to lead the team on the field, and the case will be brought into the attention of the Town Commission, Regional Commission or the Central Hockey Commission.

Article sixty one.
INSULTING LANGUAGE
a) It is forbidden for the player to address insults to the colleagues, adversaries, as well as to the public.

b) Not respecting this rule attracts the punishment for unfair attitude.

Article sixty two.
UNFAIR ATTITUDE
If the referee determines that a player, coach or leader has an unfair attitude, he can stop the game. He will eliminate from the game the one that made the mistake.

Note. *The player, coach or team leader eliminated will have to leave the field's precinct.*

Article sixty three.
REPAIRING THE EQUIPMENT
a) If a player suffers damages to his skates or equipment, the game will not be stopped.

b) The player that stops the puck for such a reason will suffer a minor penalty.

c) The player is responsible for the good state of his equipment. In the case when the skates or equipment of the player suffered damages, he must leave the ice at once, being replaced without the game stopping.

d) This rule does not apply to the goalkeeper, which can, when the game is stopped, to ask permission to the referee for the time-out time to be extended until he repairs his equipment or skate. Not respecting this rule by the goalkeeper attracts a minor penalty.

Article sixty four.
BREAKING THE HOCKEY STICK

a) A player without a hockey stick cannot participate at the game. In the case a player's hockey stick broke, he can continue playing with the remaining part and with the obligation to dispose of it at once he is not in the possession of the puck anymore. Breaking this rule attracts a minor penalty.

b) The goalkeeper can continue playing with a broken hockey stick until the game stops, when he will receive a new one.

Note. *The broken hockey stick is the one that in the referee's opinion does not correspond to continuing a normal game.*

c) The player whose hockey stick broke cannot receive another hockey stick that is thrown to him on the ice, from any part of the skating rink. The player must go personally to the players' bench to take himself another hockey stick.

The goalkeeper cannot receive the hockey stick that is thrown from outside the field. In the case he needs another hockey stick, he is not forced to go personally to the players' bench, but a team colleague can bring it to him. A penalty for unfair attitude, to which is added a minor penalty, is applied to the player or goalkeeper that receives a hockey stick in irregular conditions.

Article sixty five.
FALLING OVER THE PUCK
a) To the player (not the goalkeeper though) that falls intentionally on the puck or hides it under his body, will be applied a minor penalty.

b) No defense player, beside the goalkeeper, has the right to throw over the puck or to keep it under him in the goalpost's territory.

c) In the case this rule is not respected the game will be stopped and will be given a penalty kick against the team that made the mistake.

Note. *This rule must be interpreted in the meaning that a penalty kick is awarded only when the puck is found in the goalpost's territory in the moment the game is stopped. In the case the puck is outside the goalpost's territory, it is applied the point a) of this rule, meaning is given a minor penalty, not a penalty kick.*

Article sixty six.
THE HOCKEY STICK HELD TOO HIGH
a) It is forbidden to hold the hockey stick higher than the shoulder's height. The player that breaks this rule will be punished with a minor penalty.

b) A point scored by a hockey stick held over the shoulder's height will not be counted, outside the case it is scored by a defense player.

c) A player that, holding the hockey stick over the shoulder's height, injures at the head a player from the adversary team will be sanctioned with a major penalty.

d) It is forbidden hitting the puck that came through the air, with the hockey stick held higher than shoulder's height. In case of mistake, the game will be interrupted, being made on the place of the mistake an engagement. It is an exception the case when a defense player, trying to stop the puck from up, inserts it in his own goalpost. In this case, the point is accepted.

Article sixty seven.
THROWING THE HOCKEY STICK

a) If a player in defense, including the goalkeeper, throws intentionally the hockey stick or a part of it toward the puck found in defense, the referee will let the game continue and if in this phase is not scored a point, will award a penalty kick in the favor of the attack team.

In the case the point is scored, is not awarded anymore the penalty kick. It will be awarded a point in the case a forerunner from the attack, found in front of the empty goalpost, without having any defender in front, shoots the goalpost but the puck is stopped to enter into the empty goalpost by the hockey stick thrown by an adversary team's player.

b) A major penalty will be awarded to the player that throws the hockey stick or a part of it in any of the field's areas, except for the case when it is penalized with a penalty kick or point.

Note. *If a player, breaking the hockey stick, throws a part of it toward the field's ball cushions (but not from the top) under the intention to get rid of the useless piece and if by throwing he does not stop the attack team's play, he will not be sanctioned.*

c) The player that will throw a hockey stick or a part of it into the bystanders will be punished with an unfair attitude penalization.

Article sixty eight.
PUSHING WITH THE BODY

a) Pushing with the body is admitted only in the back of the red line, meaning, for each team, in his own half of the field.

b) To the player, that flings over an adversary team's player and pushes him incorrectly, will be applied a minor penalty.

c) To the player that attacks irregular a goalkeeper, when he is in the goalpost's space, will be applied a major penalty.

d) To the player that jumps over a player of the adversary team or pushes him from behind, will be applied a major penalty.

Note. *An irregular attack is the one executed with a greater avidness than two steps.*

Article sixty nine.
PUSHED AT THE BALL CUSHION
To the player that pushes violently in the ball cushion a player from the adversary team, either this push is made with the body, with the hockey stick or with the elbow, it will be applied to him, after the referee's opinion, a minor or major penalty.

Article seventy.
THE INCORRECT STOP OF A PLAYER
To the player that holds a player from the adversary team with his hand, with the hockey stick or in any other way, will be applied a minor penalty.

Article seventy one.
OBSTRUCTIONS
a) It will be applied a minor penalty to the player that stops another player from the adversary team, that in not in the possession of the puck, stopping him to move, throwing his hockey stick or tripping him, if he dropped his hockey stick, to stop him pick it up,-will be punished with a minor penalty.

Note. *The last player that touched the puck, outside the goalkeeper, must be considered to own the puck. Applying this rule, the referee must appreciate which is the player that makes* *the obstruction. It happens many times that the action of moving of the player in attack to be cause of the obstruction, because the defense players have the right to hold their place when the attack players score. The team colleagues of the player that holds the puck, are not allowed to help him, stopping the defense players in their attempt to stop the puck.*

b) A player from the attack that does not own the puck, does not have the right to stand on the goalpost's line, in the goalpost space or to hold the hockey stick inside this space, as long as the puck is no longer in the goalpost's space. If it is scored a point in these conditions, it will not be awarded and an engagement will happen in the neutral area in the nearest point from the attack line of the mistaking team.

c) If an attack player is pushed intentionally by a defense player in the goalpost's space, in these conditions being scored a point, it will be awarded.

Article seventy two.
STOPPING OR CAUSING THE FALL OF A PLAYER FROM THE ADVERSARY TEAM

a) The player that stops or causes the fall of a player from the adversary team using for this purpose the hockey stick, the knees, the leg, the arm, hand or the elbow, will be punished with a minor penalty.

Note. *The player that causes involuntary the fall of an adversary, dispossessing him by the puck will not be penalized.*

b) If a player has the puck, in front opposing to him only the goalkeeper, and a player from defense stops him to shoot the goalpost, throwing his or putting him in the situation to lose his balance, it will be awarded against the team that made the mistake a penalization kick. Still, the referee stops the game, only in the case when the attack team loses the puck.

Note. *To own the puck means to lead it with the hockey stick. If while it is led this way the puck touches an adversary*
48

player or the goalpost's poles, evading to the player, it is no longer counted as being in the possession of the puck. This article follows to give the possibility to the team in attack, which is irregularly stopped to score, to be able to obtain the point after all. This is why the rule tells that if exist normal possibilities to obtain the point, the sanction of penalization kick to not be awarded.

Article seventy three.
ELBOW HITS
To the player that uses his elbow to push an adversary team' player, will be applied a major penalty.

Article seventy four.
PUSHING WITH THE HOCKEY STICK
a) To the player that pushes an adversary with the hockey stick, hits him with its handle or blade, will be applied a minor penalty.

b) To the player that makes such a mistake, injuring his adversary, will be applied a major penalty.

Note. *To push with the hockey stick means to hold the hockey stick with both hands, without it touching the ice, and this way to be pushed a player from the adversary team. Also, it is forbidden pushing an adversary, touching him with the blade of the hockey stick, either the hockey stick is held with one hand or with both.*

Article seventy five.
CLENCHING WITH THE HOCKEY STICK
a) To the player that stops or tries to stop the movement of a player from the adversary team, clenching him with the hockey stick, will be applied a minor penalty.

b) To the player that doing as such, injuries a player from the adversary team, will be applied a major penalty.

Article seventy six.
HITTING WITH THE HOCKEY STICK

a) To the player that stops a player from the adversary team to move forward, hitting him with the hockey stick, will be applied a major penalty.

b) To the player that doing as such injures a player from the adversary team, will be applied a match penalty. Replacing the guilty one will be made after five minutes of playing.

Article seventy seven.
FEET KICKS

The player that hits or tries to hit using his leg a player from the adversary team, will be punished with match penalty. The guilty can be replaced only after five minutes of playing.

Article seventy eight.
EXCHANGE OF KICKS

a) To the player that starts hitting with his fist, will be applied a match penalty.

b) To the player that being hit responds or tries to respond with hits will be applied a major penalty. Replacing of the guilty will be made only after five minutes of playing.

c) To the player that participates at an exchange of hits outside the playing field will be applied an unfair attitude penalty.

Article seventy nine.
THE PLAYERS THAT LEAVE THE PLAYERS' OR PENALIZED' BENCH

a) It is forbidden to any player to leave the player's bench to be part of a conflict.

b) The player that will break this rule, will receive an unfair attitude penalty.

c) It is forbidden for the penalized player to leave the penalized bench before the end of the half time or before the end of the punishment.

d) It will be added a minor penalty to the initial punishment of the penalized player, which left the penalization bench before the end of his punishment, either the game is interrupted or not, even though he is not part of the dispute.

e) It will be added a minor penalty at the unfair attitude penalization of a penalized player, which leaves the penalization bench to be part of a dispute.

f) If a player leaves the penalization bench before the end of the punishment, the penalty time clerk will announce the referee immediately.

g) If a player reenters on the ice because of a mistake of the penalty time clerk, before the penalty is over, the player will not receive a new punishment but will have to complete the time of the punishment interrupted.

h) If an attack player, owning the puck, is found in front of the goalpost in the situation he only has in front the goalkeeper, but he is stopped by a player of adversary team entered on ice in irregular conditions, the referee will grant a penalty kick against the team the player that made the mistake is part of.

i) The leader or the coach that enters on the ice during the game without the permission of the referee, will be suspended on the entire duration of the game and will no longer have the right to lead the team from the players' bench. The referee will mention this diversion in the arbitrage chart.

Article eighty.
INJURY ATTEMPTS
Against any player that tries intentionally to hurt a player of the adversary team, a secretary-referee or a coach, will be pronounced a match penalty. The replacement of the punished

will be made only after five minutes of playing. The case will be mentioned in the arbitrage chart.

Article eighty one.
INTENTIONED INJURIES
a) Against any player that intentionally injures a player from the adversary team, a secretary-referee, a coach or a spectator, will be pronounced a match penalty.

b) The replacement of the punished player can be made after ten minutes from the sentence of the punishment.

Article eighty two.
BRUTALITIES
Against the player guilty of brutality, it will be pronounced a minor penalty.

Article eighty three.
THE SPECTATOR'S INTERVENTION
a) Is a player is stopped by a spectator to play the puck, the game will be stopped. If the team of the player involved enters in the possession of the puck, the game will not be stopped. In the case of stopping the puck will be made an engagement on the place where the puck has been played, before the spectator's intervention.

b) If the spectators throw objects on the ice, which can stop the game, the referee will stop the game and will give after an engagement on the spot where the game was stopped.

CPSIA information can be obtained
at www.ICGtesting.com
Printed in the USA
BVHW042101170621
609884BV00016B/157